Going Ape!

By Eduardo Bustos   Illustrated by Lucho Rodríguez

TUNDRA BOOKS

Published in Canada by Tundra Books
75 Sherbourne Street, Toronto, Ontario M5A 2P9

Published in the United States by Tundra Books of Northern New York
P.O. Box 1030, Plattsburgh, New York 12901

Library of Congress Control Number: 2011923289

Library and Archives Canada Cataloguing in Publication

Bustos, Eduardo
       Going ape! / by Eduardo Bustos ; illustrated by Lucho Rodríguez.

Translation of: ¡Que monos!
ISBN 978-1-77049-282-0

       1. Monkeys – Juvenile literature. 2. Picture books for
children. I. Rodríguez, Lucho II. Title.

QL737.P9B88 2012   j599.8   C2011-901403-3

We acknowledge the financial support of the Government of Canada through the Book
Publishing Industry Development Program (BPIDP) and that of the Government of Ontario
through the Ontario Media Development Corporation's Ontario Book Initiative.

We further acknowledge the support of the Canada Council for the Arts and the Ontario
Arts Council for our publishing program.

ONTARIO ARTS COUNCIL
CONSEIL DES ARTS DE L'ONTARIO

Printed and bound in China

1 2 3 4 5 6   17 16 15 14 13 12

Going Ape!

Apes come in different colors
and shapes, sit in curious poses,
and make trees their homes.

BABOON:

The baboon climbs
to the top of the tree
to meet his troop. His
rosy bottom allows
him to sleep upright
without falling.

CHIMPANZEE:

The chimpanzee is very clever. He can make tools and use them for gathering food. He can even build nests in trees!

GIBBON:

This little ape has no tail, but he doesn't seem to miss it. He lives in a tropical rainforest and is the fastest mammal that lives in trees and cannot fly.

GORILLA:

The mighty gorilla lives
in Central Africa. He
gets around by knuckle-
walking. The gorilla is
strong and powerful.
When he is angry,
stay away.

JAPANESE MACAQUE:

He dips in hot springs to keep warm and even washes his food. The macaque is known for being a great swimmer and can swim more than half a kilometer.

MANGABEY:

This colorful monkey is sometimes called "four-eyed" because he has bright white eyelids. The mangabey can be very noisy because he has a large throat-sac.

ALLEN'S SWAMP MONKEY:

This elegant gray monkey is no bigger than a small dog. Because he lives in a swamp, his webbed feet are very useful.

DE BRAZZA'S MONKEY:

The De Brazza's Monkey looks like a bearded old man. When frightened, he curls up into a ball to hide.

SACRED BABOON:

The Sacred Baboon got his name from the ancient Egyptians, who thought he was sacred. Strangely enough, he is no longer found in Egypt.

ORANGUTAN:

The orangutan takes
a long time to mature.
Young orangutans live
with their mothers for
seven years.

There are more than two hundred primates (mammals with hands, handlike feet, and forward-facing eyes) on our planet, and, with the exception of humans, they are all known as apes. Very few people know much about these creatures, which are so similar to us. In fact, they might not even know their names!

There are apes of every size. The tiniest is the Pygmy Marmoset, which fits into the palm of your hand, and the largest, the gorilla, weighs about two hundred kilograms.

Monkeys come in a range of colors, sometimes in an orange color, like the orangutan, or green like the green monkey. Others have distinctive colors on their faces, such as the Japanese macaque, or on their backsides, such as the baboon. Some have short hair, others have long.

It is interesting to learn about their habits. Unlike most animals, apes use their hands to eat. Depending on the species, their favorite foods include leaves, fruit, insects, and occasionally meat.

They also form their families in different ways. The Sacred Baboon prefers to have many partners, while the gibbon chooses to have one. The mothers take care of the babies for at least a year, providing food and shelter.

Primates are fascinating creatures!

[9]